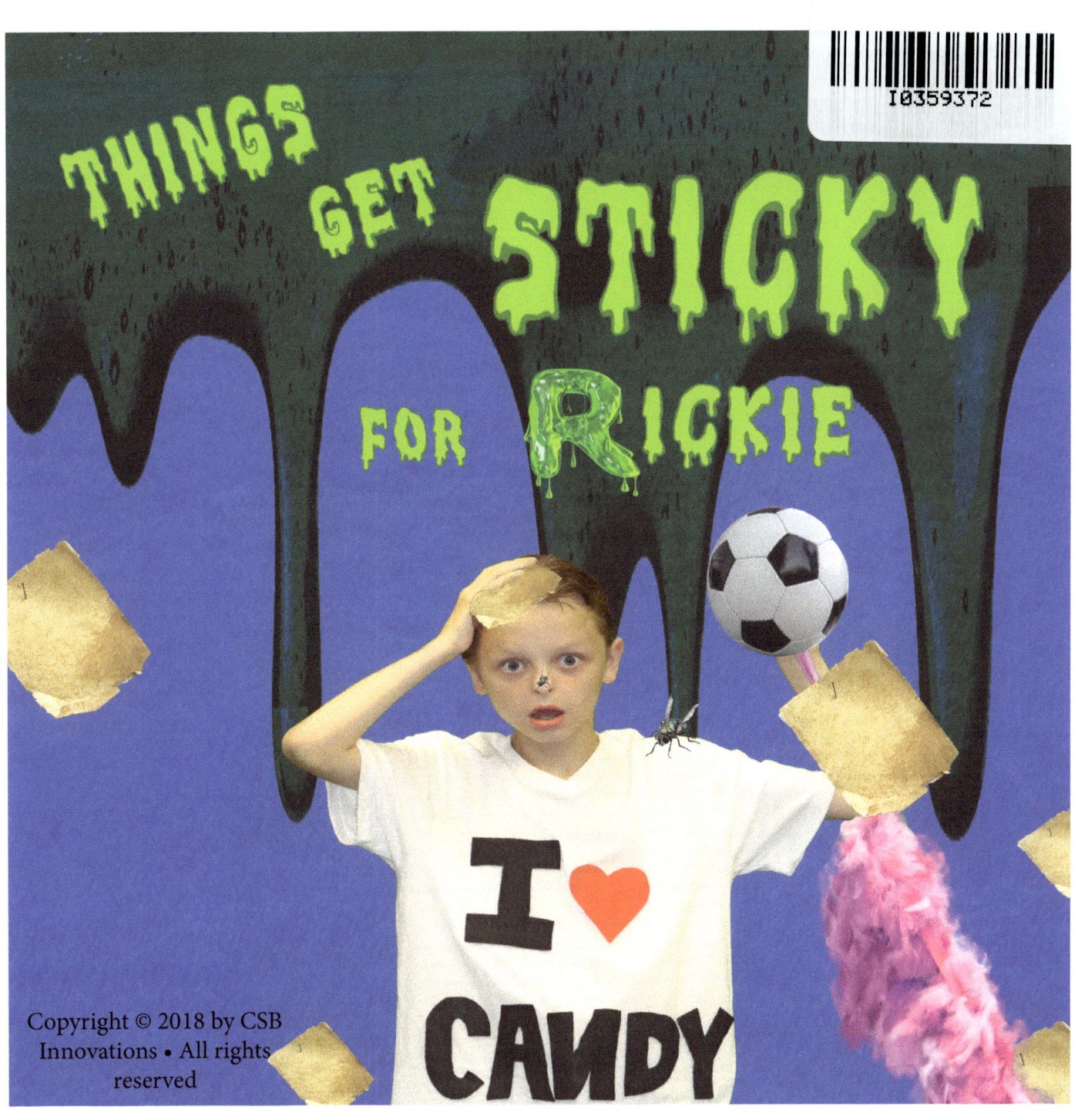

THIS THRILLING SUMPKINVILLE TALE

is about a boy named Rickie, whose life one-day got very sticky!

Wunchbarz, Twizzlebars, Skelopop, Pumpkinpops and, of course, Sumpkinvilles famous Mucshok chocolate bars. No matter the name or flavor of the candies, Rickie loves them all.

Today is a very exciting day because, on Wednesdays, Rickie and his mom visit the Candy Store.
Rickie just loves to look at all the candy in the store, and sometimes his mom even buys him a piece of candy.

As his mom tells Rickie that it's time to leave the store, Rickie begs his mom for his favorite, a Wunchbar.

But she replies, "No, Rickie, not today. Too much candy will make your teeth rot away."

Rickie is not happy with this news, and he knows just what to do!
"Surely one Wunchbar won't be missed," thinks Rickie. So just as Miss Raspberry looks the other way, Rickie takes a Wunchbarz and then leaves the store.

Ready to play, Rickie heads to the Soccer field where he sees his good friend, Seth. Seth is excited to see him and, with a big smile, waves hi to Rickie.

Seth asks Rickie to play soccer with him, and Rickie agrees, excited Seth kicks the ball toward Rickie. Rickie tries to kick it back, but the ball sticks to his foot!

"Oh no!" Rickie shouts, "it's stuck, the ball is stuck to my foot!" Seth runs over to help Rickie; he pulls out a spatula from one of the pockets from his shirt and tries to pry the ball off of Rickie's foot, but no matter how hard Rickie and Seth try, the ball won't come off of Rickie's foot.

Hoping the ball will come off on his own, Rickie heads to the park where he sees Sas-lah walking her sassy dog.

"Hi Sas-lah, what are you doing?" asks Rickie.
"I'm walking my dog, HELLO," replies Sas-lah.

"Why is there a soccer ball stuck to your foot?" asks Sas-lah.
"I don't know," says Rickie. "I was playing soccer with Seth, but when I tried to kick the ball back, it just stuck."

"Hold my dog while I try to take it off, "says Sas-lah.
Sas-lah pulls and tugs as much as she can, but the soccer ball just won't budge.

"Sorry, Rickie, I can't get it off.
Can you give me back Sassy now?

Rickie tries to hand her Sassy back when he realizes that he can't.

Just like the ball, Rickie is now stuck with Sas-lah's dog!

With the soccer ball stuck to his foot and a Sassy dog in his hand, a confused Rickie wanders around .

When suddenly a gust of wind brings trash with it, and now Rickie has trash stuck on his head.

Rickie decides that he needs to fix this sticky mess, so he heads to Mike Bonicors, a local janitor and inventor. Mike welcomes him in and invites him to be the first to sit on his latest invention, a Toilet Chair.

As Rickie sits, he tells Mike about his sticky mess.
Mike suggests, "Rickie, perhaps you should talk to your mom about this sticky mess."

Rickie agrees and tries to get up to leave, but he can't!

Using the R.A.D. machine (Robotic Arm Device),
Mike removes the toilet cover from his toilet chair,
and giggles a little as he watches
Rickie walk out the door.

With a toilet chair cover stuck to his bottom, trash stuck on his head, a ball stuck on his foot, and a sassy dog stuck to his hand, Rickie decides to take Mike's advice and talk to his mom.

THE CANDY CURSE

Rickie's mom tells him about the curse on the Candy Store, "Children who steal will be revealed, and the only way out of this sticky mess is to confess."

So to the Candy store, Rickie goes to confess and apologize for his mistakes and promise never again to take something that doesn't belong to him.
Mrs. Raspberry accepts his apology and watches as Rickie dances for joy when he realizes that he no longer has anything stuck to him

Contributing Authors

KENEDY LIBRARY
Contributing Authors

Lola Jane Aragon

Lola Jane Aragon is 7 years old and on her way to 2nd grade. She is brilliant and has a creative imagination. She is always praised for being a great leader, helper, and a role model. She enjoys reading, playing baseball, swimming in her pool, and spending quality time with her family. Being the oldest of 3, she gives her younger siblings a positive outlook to shoot for the stars and follow your dreams.

Owen Friesen

Owen Friesen is 10 years old. He wants to be an astronaut and be among the first to live on Mars. He loves reading more than anything, and also enjoys Lego, being creative, playing video games, doing Tae Kwon Do and writing his own books at home.

KENEDY LIBRARY
CONTRIBUTING AUTHORS

Jaxson M. Singleton

Jaxson M. Singleton is 9 years old and wants to be a Lego set creator when he grows up. He loves to read, watch Star Wars movies, and spending time with his family. Jaxson trusts in Jesus as his savior and loves being part of his church.

Mckenzie Gonzales

Mckenzie Gonzales is 9 years old with aspirations of being an obstetrician. She is part of the gifted and talented program at Roger E. Sides Elementary. She loves to write and draw.

KENEDY LIBRARY
Contributing Authors

Catherine M. Quintanilla

Catherine M. Quintanilla is 12 years old and wants to be a neonatal surgeon when she grows up. Catherine enjoys playing volleyball, spending quality time with her family and her dogs. She is a gifted and talented student; she loves school and always strives to do her best in all she does. Catherine is loving, caring, and she has a kind heart

Ozzy Martinez

Ozzy is 10 years old (almost 11). He loves to read, walk, and is very active in his school and church. He has always had an interest in acting, magic, dancing, and science experiments. He is a very kind and loving Christian and loves to play outside, and with his sister.

KENEDY LIBRARY
Contributing Authors

Raimani J. Wilcox

Raimani J. Wilcox is 6 years old and wants to be a beluga whale trainer when he grows up. He loves to play every sport there is, he dances all the time, loves the outdoors, video games, and spending time with his big brothers. Raimani is the sweetest, most respectful boy who loves learning and being around family and friends.

Izaiah Maldorado

Izaiah Maldorado is a 7-year-old energetic and creative boy. He loves to read, draw, play video games and baseball. Izaiah also loves to watch wrestling and write stories of his own at home. When Izaiah is not at school, he is home playing with his sister of having movie nights at home with his family.

KENEDY LIBRARY
Contributing Authors

Nathaniel Friesen

Nathaniel Friesen is 8 years old. He loves Lego, being creative, swimming, playing video games and writing his own comics at home. As a dual citizen, he wants to be the Prime Minister of Canada and then the President of the United States.

Deven E. Martinez

Deven E. Martinez is 6 years old and wants to be a game designer on some days and an art teacher on other days when he grows up. He enjoys creating his own comics, flip books, and he also likes to collect coins. Deven is a sweet boy with big dreams.

KENEDY LIBRARY
CONTRIBUTING AUTHORS

Wilson Friesen

Wilson Friesen is 9 years old and wants to be a zoologist working with giraffes when he grows up. He loves Lego, reading, playing video games, swimming, and doing Tae Kwan Do.

Fan Pages

CHARACTERS

Shomari G. Wilcox is 12 years old and wants to play in the NBA when he grows up. He loves to play basketball, video games, and spending time with both his brothers. Shomari is kindhearted and very respectful to everyone. He also loves to spend time with family and friends.

Shomari G. Wilcox

Chylah Jae Gonzales is 7 years old and wants to be a veterinarian when she grows up. Chylah is kind and has a big heart when it comes to others. She loves to bake and play outside.

Chylah Jae Gonzales

CHARACTERS

Benjamin "AYDEN" Arriola is an intelligent energetic 12 year old boy who wants to be a scientist when he grows up! He likes basketball and football but also loves fishing and hunting. He is very compeitive both althetically and academically!! He enjoys reading at church, BBQ'S with the family and being a big brother.

BENJAMIN ARRIOLA

John Friesen is 10 years old. One day, he wants to serve as an emergency responder as a policeman, firefighter, or search and rescue worker. He loves Legos, playing video games, reading and working hard.

JOHN FRIESEN

www.csbinnovations.com

www.ingramcontent.com/pod-product-compliance
Lightning Source LLC
Chambersburg PA
CBHW040044100526
44584CB00033BA/4270